THE COSMIC CRIMINAL

WORKBOOK

THE COSMIC CRIMINAL

WORKBOOK

CAROLYN CHAMBERS

KEITH CHAMBERS

The Cosmic Criminal - *Workbook*

Carolyn Chambers

Keith Chambers

© Copyright 2018 by Carolyn & Keith Chambers. All rights reserved. Unless otherwise indicated, all scripture quotations are taken from the King James Version of the Bible, except when indicated.

Definitions-Webster's 1828 Dictionary.

No portion of this book may be reproduced, stored in a retrieval system or transmitted in any form electronic, mechanical, photocopy, recording or any other except for brief quotations in printed reviews, without prior consent of the publisher.

Library of Congress Cataloging-in-Publication Data

The Cosmic Criminal - Workbook

Printed in the United States of America
ISBN: 978-0-9967582-7-7

Cover design by CW Technology Consulting

www.anointedlifepublishing.com

TABLE OF CONTENTS

The Enemies of Grace Review 1
The Processes of Grace Review 15
The Wager Against Grace 33
Ahab's Case Against Grace 35
    House Divided 37
    Not Fully Persuaded 39
    Your Reasonable Service 41
    Confessions of Faith 43
    The Accuser of the Brethren 45
    On Guard 47
    Don't Tap Out 49
Conclusion: Don't Blame God 53
Epilogue 57
Answers to Questions 59
About the Authors 67

And from the days of John the Baptist until now the kingdom of heaven suffered violence, and the violent take it by force.

(Matthew 11:12 KJV)

Fight Back!

The Enemies of Grace Review

This companion workbook begins by examining the enemies of grace that were discussed in the book: *The Cosmic Criminal*. In that *book,* we learned that our fall from grace creates breaches, infractions of God's law. These breaches give place to the enemy. We are then alienated from the very grace that was sent to deliver us. This of course, affects our ability to fulfill the call of God on our lives; as well as our ability to possess our possessions.

In Chapters 1-6, of *The Cosmic Criminal*, we focused on six enemies of grace. These enemies seek to pervert the right ways of God:

- o Perception: Our Own Mental Image
- o Unbelief: Believing Something God Did Not Say
- o Fear: An Expectation of Evil; Little Faith
- o Care: Concern, Anxiety, and Caution
- o Doubt: To Waver, to Question, to Suspect, to Withhold Confidence, Dread, and to Distrust
- o Pleasant Knowledge: Knowledge Pleasant to the Soul

Knowing these enemies of grace will level the playing field—so that you will not be caught off guard.

In this *section* of the workbook, you will find study questions in each of the areas listed above. These questions are designed to reinforce your wisdom and deepen your understanding of each concept. As you seek to 'know them by heart,' they will be a present help for you in your time of need.

Fight the good fight of faith, lay hold on eternal life, whereunto thou art also called, and hast professed a good profession before many witnesses.

(1 Timothy 6:12)

It is a good fight because we win.

Complete the reading assignment and then answer the following to the best of your knowledge. All questions refer to chapters in **The Cosmic Criminal.** The answer key is located in the back of this book.

Read Chapter 1: **'Grace vs. Perception'**

a.   What manner of grace did King David offer to Hanun?

_____

_____

_____

b.   What was Hanun's case against grace?

_____

_____

_____

c.   When do you have to litigate by scripture?

_____

_____

_____

d. According to the author, when do 'breaches' occur?

_____

_____

_____

e. How does the enemy react when we fall from grace?

_____

_____

_____

f. What does 'King to king' business mean?

_____

_____

_____

Notes:

_____

_____

_____

_____.

Complete the reading assignment and then answer the following to the best of your knowledge. All questions refer to chapters in **The Cosmic Criminal.** The answer key is located in the back of <u>this</u> book.

Read Chapter 2: **'Grace vs. Unbelief'**

a. At the pool of Bethesda, what was the man's case against grace?

___

b. How is *unbelief* initially received?

___

c. How does unbelief affect our conscience?

___

d. In Luke 15, what decision did the son make before returning to his father's house?

_____

_____

_____

e. What factor(s) hinder the flow of grace?

_____

_____

_____

Notes:

_____

_____

_____

_____

_____

_____

_____.

Complete the reading assignment and then answer the following to the best of your knowledge. All questions refer to chapters in **The Cosmic Criminal.** The answer key is located in the back of this book.

Read Chapter 3: **'Grace vs. Fear'**

a.   What was Elijah's case against grace?

_____

_____

_____

b.   Who was Jezebel, and how was she involved with Elijah?

_____

_____

_____

c.   How did God redeem Elijah?

_____

_____

_____

d. Why did the angel call Gideon a mighty man of valor?

_____

_____

_____

Notes:

_____

_____

_____

_____

_____

_____

_____

_____

_____

_____

_____.

Complete the reading assignment and then answer the following to the best of your knowledge. All questions refer to chapters in ***The Cosmic Criminal.*** The answer key is located in the back of <u>this</u> book.

Read Chapter 4: **'Grace vs. Care'**

a.   What was Martha's case against grace?

_____

_____

_____

b.   How did Daniel remain faithful to God when the men plotted against him?

_____

_____

_____

c.   What is the 'flood attack?'

_____

_____

_____

d. Why is it important for us to 'stand?'

_____

_____

_____

Notes:

Complete the reading assignment and then answer the following to the best of your knowledge. All questions refer to chapters in *The Cosmic Criminal.* The answer key is located in the back of this book.

Read Chapter 5: **'Grace vs. Doubt'**

a.   What was the author's case against grace?

_____

_____

_____

b.   What are some of the impacts of doubt on our minds?

_____

_____

_____

c.   What happens when we are bound by doubt?

_____

_____

_____

_____

d. What often happens when doubt challenges areas where our abilities are untested?

_____

_____

_____

e. How is doubt resisted?

_____

_____

_____

Notes:

_____

_____

_____

_____

_____

_____.

Complete the reading assignment and then answer the following to the best of your knowledge. All questions refer to chapters in *The Cosmic Criminal.* The answer key is located in the back of <u>this</u> book.

Read Chapter 6: **'Grace vs. Pleasant Knowledge'**

a. What was Ammon's case against grace?

_____

_____

_____

b. What was Tamar's 'way out' for Ammon?

_____

_____

_____

c. Why did Ammon not take Tamar's 'way out?'

_____

_____

_____

d. According to the Pleasant Knowledge Alert, how is pleasant knowledge defined?

_____

_____

_____

Notes:

_____

_____

_____

_____

_____

_____

_____

_____

_____

_____.

The Processes of Grace Review

In Chapter 7, of **The Cosmic Criminal,** we focused on seven processes of grace. Below you will also see a snapshot of their breaches; stumbling blocks. These breaches show us were we have missed the mark (the standard of grace that we failed to lift up).

- Grace to Discern-   breach: undetected falsehood
- Grace to Overcome-   breach: unbought field
- Grace to Occupy-   breach: unclaimed goods
- Grace to Pray-   breach: unfaithfulness
- Grace to Dominate-   breach: ungoverned mind
- Grace to Watch-   breach: untroubled flesh
- Grace to Sow-   breach: unencouraged heart

In this *section* of the workbook, you will find study questions in each of the areas listed above. These questions are designed to reinforce your wisdom and deepen your understanding of each concept. As you seek to 'know them by heart,' they will enable you to hit the mark.

…Not by might, nor by power, but by my spirit, saith the LORD of hosts…Grace, grace unto it...

(Zechariah 4:6-9)

You can't do it alone!

Complete the reading assignment and then answer the following to the best of your knowledge. All questions refer to **chapter 7 sub-chapters** in *The Cosmic Criminal*. The answer key is located in the back of <u>this</u> book.

Read **'Grace to Discern'** in chapter 7.

a.   How did Abraham begin to tap into his spiritual inheritance?

_____

_____

_____

b.   What statement did Abraham make to demonstrate that he had tapped into the will of God?

_____

_____

_____

c.   What was the heaven to earth agreement between God and Adam, regarding Eve?

_____

_____

_____

d. What does the process of 'Calling and Naming' guard?

_____

_____

e. What 'mistake' did King Joash make when he only smote upon the ground three times?

_____

_____

_____

f. What warning did God give to the Israelites regarding the inhabitants of the land, in the book of Numbers?

_____

_____

_____

Notes:

_____

_____

_____

_____.

Complete the reading assignment and then answer the following to the best of your knowledge. All questions refer to chapter **7 sub-chapters** in *The Cosmic Criminal*. The answer key is located in the back of <u>this</u> book.

Read **'Grace to Overcome'** in chapter 7.

a. What does 'Buying and Selling' refer to?

_____

_____

_____

b. Explain Mary's reasoning, regarding her spirit, based on her statement in Luke 1:46-47.

_____

_____

_____

c. What did the 'wise' virgins do that the 'foolish' ones did not do?

_____

_____

_____

d. What does the 'field' represent regarding 'buying and selling?'

_____

_____

_____

e. What is required to 'buy' the field?

_____

_____

_____

Notes:

_____

_____

_____

_____

_____

_____

_____

_____.

Complete the reading assignment and then answer the following to the best of your knowledge. All questions refer to **chapter 7 sub-chapters** in ***The Cosmic Criminal.*** The answer key is located in the back of <u>this</u> book.

Read **'Grace to Occupy'** in chapter 7.

a.   What does 'Grace to Occupy' represent?

_____

_____

_____

b.   How did the Rechabites occupy the word spoken to them by their father?

_____

_____

_____

c.   How do 'hearers and doers' and 'hearers only,' differ?

_____

_____

_____

d. What err did the man, spoken of in Matthew 7:26 make?

_____

_____

_____

e. How did his err reflect the 'reasonable service' standard?

_____

_____

_____

Notes:

_____

_____

_____

_____

_____

_____.

Complete the reading assignment and then answer the following to the best of your knowledge. All questions refer to **chapter 7 sub-chapters** in *The Cosmic Criminal*. The answer key is located in the back of this book.

Read **'Grace to Pray'** in chapter 7.

a.   What does 'Grace to Pray' represent?

_____

_____

_____

b.   What weapon does the enemy use against the 'Grace to Pray?'

_____

_____

_____

c.   In Mark 11, what did the enemy use the fig tree for, as it related to Jesus?

_____

_____

_____

d. What did Jesus teach His disciples regarding overcoming doubt?

_____

_____

_____

e. How does God respond when we do not forgive those who trespass against us?

_____

_____

_____

f. When we sin and miss the mark, what gives all believers one more move?

_____

_____

_____

Notes:

_____

_____

_____.

Complete the reading assignment and then answer the following to the best of your knowledge. All questions refer to **chapter 7 sub-chapters** in *The Cosmic Criminal*. The answer key is located in the back of this book.

Read **'Grace to Dominate'** in chapter 7.

a.   What does 'Grace to Dominate' guard, and what is its focus?

_____

_____

_____

b.   What is the redemptive name of the woman who was bowed and unable to lift herself up?

_____

_____

_____

c.   Without the Kingdom of God, where does the 'sin nature' lead us?

_____

_____

_____

d. What does Hebrews 12:14-15, say about peace?

_____

_____

_____

e. According to the author, what does 'binding and loosing' mean?

_____

_____

_____

Notes:

Complete the reading assignment and then answer the following to the best of your knowledge. All questions refer to **chapter 7 sub-chapters** in *The Cosmic Criminal*. The answer key is located in the back of <u>this</u> book.

Read **'Grace to Watch'** in chapter 7.

a. What does 'Grace to Watch' refer to?

_____

_____

_____

b. In the movie, *Wait Until Dark*, what was the heroine's key to victory?

_____

_____

_____

c. In 1 Kings 13, how did the 'man of God' disobey God?

_____

_____

_____

d. In 1 Kings 13, what happened to the man of God following his disobedience?

_____
_____
_____

Notes:

Complete the reading assignment and then answer the following to the best of your knowledge. All questions refer to **chapter 7 sub-chapters** in *The Cosmic Criminal*. The answer key is located in the back of <u>this</u> book.

Read **'Grace to Sow'** in chapter 7.

a. How did David's men sow to their flesh after the Amalekites plundered their land?

_____

_____

_____

b. According to Galatians 6:7-9, when do we reap the harvest?

_____

_____

_____

c. According to Galatians 6:7-9, what will stop the harvest?

_____

_____

_____

d. According to Matthew 25:14-30, why was the last servant unprofitable?

_____

_____

_____

Notes:

_____

_____

_____

_____

_____

_____

_____

_____

_____

_____

_____.

Complete the reading assignment and then answer the following to the best of your knowledge. All questions refer to **chapter 8** in *The Cosmic Criminal.* The answer key is located in the back of <u>this</u> book.

Read '**Possessing your Possessions**' in chapter 8.

a.   What was the army of Israel's case against grace?

_____

_____

_____

b.   How did David pass his 'perverseness test?'

_____

_____

_____

c.   Who did the Israelites leave out of the equation?

_____

_____

_____

d. What is the shout of a king?

_____

_____

_____

Notes:

_____

_____

_____

_____

_____

_____

_____

_____

_____

_____

_____.

The Wager Against Grace

Now, we will turn our attention to the wager that is launched <u>against the execution</u> of the processes of grace.

The wager, of the enemies of grace, is that the seven processes of grace will be executed *in reverse*. Their bet is that we will: fail to discern truth from falsehood; lose our joy and not overcome; not occupy the Word so that they may instead occupy our goods; confess our fears, doubts, and unbelief and not our faith; not set a watch as they watch to slay us; sow to the flesh and not sow to the Spirit.

But, they lose, hands down. The key lies in our commitment: to **fight back** (confess our faith); to **receive an instruction contrary to our own thoughts** (follow the leading of our spirit); and to **stand** (in our place of authority).

In the Cosmic Criminal, we saw how David applied all seven processes of grace and was triumphant over Goliath.

We will now examine how our failure to apply these processes changes our outcome. This will be from the perspective of King Ahab. As we chronicle the last days of King Ahab's life, we will evaluate the steps that Ahab took that led to his early demise. You will see how he unilaterally violated all seven processes of grace; and instead, he yielded to the enemies of grace. In each occurrence, he failed to fight back, even though the stakes were high.

Verily, verily, I say unto you, Except a corn of wheat fall into the ground and die, it abideth alone: but if it die, it bringeth forth much fruit.

(John 12:24)

We must be willing to change our perspective.

Ahab's Case Against Grace

In 2 Chronicles 18, the story is told of two kings: Jehoshaphat and Ahab. Jehoshaphat—the good king—joined affinity with Ahab, who the Bible describes as evil. King Ahab made plans to go to battle for the city of Ramoth-gilead, and he persuaded King Jehoshaphat to go with him. Jehoshaphat agreed, but he received a divine influence of grace, and he asked if they could first seek God's will regarding the matter.

Then King Ahab gathered his four hundred *personal* prophets and they, all in one accord, said, "Go up; for God will deliver it into the king's hand." But Jehoshaphat said, "Is there not here a prophet of the Lord...?" The king said, yes but that he hated him because he never prophesied good, but always evil. Nonetheless, Ahab is persuaded to ask anyway.

The Prophet of God eventually told the king that it was not God's will to go up. Then Ahab said, "Did I not tell thee *that* he would not prophesy good unto me, but evil?" Ahab then imprisoned the prophet, saying, "...Until I return in peace." Ahab refused to buy the truth and made the decision to go up to Ramoth-gilead, anyway. As a safety precaution, he decided to disguise himself. Sadly, Ahab was wounded in the battle and later died.

In the following pages, we will analyze each of the seven processes of grace and pinpoint the breaches that led to Ahab's down-fall:

- Process 1: Grace to Discern
- Process 2: Grace to Overcome
- Process 3: Grace to Occupy
- Process 4: Grace to Pray
- Process 5: Grace to Dominate
- Process 6: Grace to Watch
- Process 7: Grace to Sow

And if a **house be divided** against itself, that house cannot stand.

(Mark 3:25)

They cannot weather the storm,

being torn by emotions.

House Divided

Grace to Discern

As you know, God desires His will to be done on earth as it is in heaven—<u>God is looking for our will to align with His</u>. If there is a misalignment of wills, we then have violated the first crucial test of agreement. We failed to <u>discern</u> truth from falsehood. This means that the spirit of man was not involved in the decision that was made. Instead, it was a soulish decision, one based: on perception, thoughts, or feelings. Decisions of this nature leave us half-hearted—unable to serve God with **all** of our heart.

King Ahab heard the will of God but he did not believe it. He aligned his will to the will of his four hundred prophets. His emotions followed; he then operated from a house divided. His spirit separated from his soul. As a result, he could not <u>discern</u> truth from falsehood. He failed to guard his will so his spirit was not involved in the decision making process. He followed his own <u>perception</u>: an enemy of grace. From that point on, every future decision would seem right but end in death. And so it was. His breach: undetected falsehood.

And being **fully persuaded** that, what he had promised, he was able also to perform.

(Romans 4:21)

The half-hearted is not fully persuaded.

Not Fully Persuaded

Grace to Overcome

As you know, God describes the kingdom of heaven as man who found treasure in a field and for joy goes and sells all that he has and buys that field. What is intimated is that the field—*the place where battles are fought*—is bought with *joy*. Good cheer redeems the field and then <u>overcomes</u> it. To <u>guard our joy</u>, this parable implies that all must be sold (surrendered). *Things that are contrary to us having joy must go*! When that has occurred, we have redeemed the field. In other words, <u>our soul is now aligned with our spirit</u>.

King Ahab's care was to get back the city of Ramoth-gilead. So when the Prophet of God told the king (in jest) what he wanted to hear, saying, "go ye up and prosper....," the king admonished him saying, *How many times shall I adjure thee that thou say nothing but the truth to me in the name of the LORD*? Then the prophet told the king the truth—that he saw Israel all scattered as sheep that had no master.

King Ahab bought the truth but *surrendered* it. He was not fully persuaded; he failed to sell all. To win, Ahab would have had to cast the care of redeeming Ramoth-gilead. However, he didn't believe that he would be defeated. After all, the odds were four hundred to one, that the Prophet of God was wrong. So, he carried that legitimate *care* into the *field*, the place where battles are fought. But not having bought the field, he could not overcome it; his soul and his spirit were misaligned. Joy could not flow. So, his doubts, fears, concerns, and cares consumed him and overcame him. His breach: an unbought field.

I beseech you therefore, brethren, by the mercies of God, that ye present your bodies a living sacrifice, holy, acceptable unto God, *which is* your **reasonable service**.

(Romans 12:1)

The body leads under the influence of the spirit.

Then we renew the mind.

Your Reasonable Service

Grace to Occupy

As you know, God has called us to present our bodies as a living sacrifice: holy, acceptable unto Him. This means that our bodies are to move under the influence of our spirit. God calls this our reasonable service. This is reasonable given that the *wisdom and knowledge of God are unsearchable, and in the natural, we can't understand His decisions and ways*. In other words, to follow the influence of our spirit is the standard of a reasonable person, given that we can't direct our own steps. To do less, is considered negligence.

It is our duty to <u>occupy</u> the Word that we have heard in our hearts. This means that we must <u>guard the Word</u> to perform it. As we occupy the Word, our bodies are free to follow the dictates of our spirit. Here, our actions are often challenged by an unrenewed mind, questioning our decisions. So, we may find ourselves defending the influences of our hearts. This is known as renewing the mind.

King Ahab neglected to occupy that *good* Word that was sown into his heart by the Prophet of God. He failed to perform it. Instead, he performed the thoughts of his own heart that was pleasant to him: *disguise yourself*. That thought caused him to be pre-occupied with his safety. He occupied that <u>fear-based</u> perception until the going down of the sun. Then he died.

If we fail to occupy God's word, the enemy will occupy the word that <u>he</u> has sown in our hearts. We will find ourselves being constantly reminded of perceptions, feelings, cares, and thoughts that he (the enemy) has planted; that were not cast down. The Bible says he will occupy our *capital goods*. Ahab's breach: unclaimed goods.

... **I believed**, and therefore have I spoken; we also believe, and therefore speak.

(2 Corinthians 4:13)

I speak my faith.

Confessions of Faith

Grace to Pray

As you know, prayer is a game changer; it is our only weapon. It will <u>guard</u> us against doubt, unbelief, care, and fear. To pray effectively, we must speak <u>words of faith</u>; your mountain needs to hear your voice. As you speak, the attack turns into a light affliction. God is not concerned about what the mountain (the attack, the enemy, the thought) is saying to you. He wants to know what you are saying to <u>it!</u> Are you fighting back? You must *consistently* confess your faith continuously; then know that as you speak, the mountain is being removed.

King Ahab confessed his <u>doubt</u>, not his faith. Being in doubt, he *consistently* confessed his suspicion of the Prophet of God saying, "Did I not tell thee *that* he would not prophesy good unto me, but evil?" Yet, the prophet of God was telling the truth. This err cost Ahab his life. Ahab also confessed that he would *return in peace*. As you know, it was a statement of unbelief, for he died from a mortal wound. His unbelief could not save him. Instead, it created <u>inconstancy</u> which could have only been remedied by grace. But the grace which could have saved his life, had been summarily, rejected. His breach: unfaithfulness.

...for the **accuser of our brethren** is <u>cast down</u>, which accused them before our God day and night.

(Revelation 12:10)

We have to <u>go down</u> to accuse another.

The Accuser of the Brethren

Grace to Dominate

As you know, we are either in our spirit or in our flesh, depending on the thoughts we receive. When we are in our spirit, it is easy to obey God. Operating from our spirit, we bind forces of darkness and loose our ministering spirits to minister on our behalf. This process of grace <u>guards the mind</u>, enabling us to bind perceptions that are contrary to our peace and wellbeing. It begins with binding (crucifying) the flesh. The flesh, being the sin nature that exalts itself against the knowledge of God, is contrary to the will of God. And, it opposes the <u>word</u> of God.

King Ahab was told by the Prophet of God that a lying spirit was sent into the mouths of his prophets to deceive him into going to battle. Being in <u>unbelief,</u> he failed to bind the lying spirit. Instead, he bound the Prophet of God and placed him in prison.

Unbelief also caused Ahab to hate the man that God had sent to save his life. Ahab had a choice: grace or hatred. God offered grace to offset the temptation of hatred. But he refused the grace (truth), and he sided with his emotions. His confession: "*I hate him,*" blinded his heart and produced a root of bitterness in him; making him an accuser of the brethren. Now many would be defiled, including: Ahab's spirit, soul, and body. His breach: an ungoverned mind.

The wicked watcheth the righteous,
and seeketh to slay him.

(Psalms 37:32)

The enemy has inside help: the wicked flesh.

On Guard

Grace to Watch

As you know, the enemy watches for a breach. If he is successful, he will attempt to occupy that breach. A breach, being defined as an infraction or a violation of the will of God, will cause us to miss God's best for our lives. This watch is especially required to avoid temptation—the temptation to change course—instead of staying the course. For this reason, we are called to guard against yielding to the flesh: our weak link. Instead, we should always guard our hearts by <u>troubling the flesh</u>. The flesh is troubled through our persistence: a refusal to give up our course.

King Ahab's plan to take back Ramoth-gilead was sound. It began as a spirit decision, but he did not persist in his course; being halfhearted was the problem. He did not know his right hand from his left; whether he was in the spirt or in the flesh. This made him unpredictable.

At any moment he could yield to his flesh and his plans could go south. That is exactly what happened. As he proceeded to go into battle, he yielded to a contaminating influence: a thought that enticed him to go in disguise. It was <u>pleasant</u> and it seemed like a good idea. However, this thought was contrary to the will of God, and it created a breach. As he acted on this thought, he was wounded. He failed to watch: to stay alert and detect the enemy from within: the flesh. As fate would have it, he *watched* the demise of his own body for the rest of that day. His breach: an untroubled flesh.

Blessed art thou, O land, when thy king is the son of nobles, and thy princes eat in ***due season***, for strength, and not for drunkenness!

(Ecclesiastes 10:17)

Don't worry, your enemy will <u>not</u> eat in due season.

Don't Tap Out

Grace to Sow

As you know, we can either sow to the Spirit or we can sow to the flesh. As we sow for the <u>harvest</u>, we will be enticed to 'tap out' (succumb to <u>weariness</u> or <u>faint</u>). Both are deceptions of the enemy designed to mock us. Those who yield to the flesh will reap corruption. They will reap the thoughts that they have sown.

King Ahab sowed to his flesh, and not to his Spirit. Even when he was wounded, he did not cry out to God for help. King Jehoshaphat, who accompanied him into battle, did. He sowed to the Spirit. He cried out for help when he was surrounded by the enemy, and God intervened on his behalf, and his life was spared. Ahab became weary in the battle, then fainted and therefore tapped out. He failed to encourage himself in the Lord. He had sown corruption and reaped the consequences of contaminating influences. His harvest (Ramoth-gilead) was lost. He missed his due season. His breach: an unencouraged heart.

Sow to yourselves in righteousness, reap in mercy; break up your fallow ground: for *it is* time to seek the LORD, till he come and rain righteousness upon you.

(Hosea 10:12)

When we seek the Lord, we reap in mercy.

I Learned:

Are ye so foolish? **Having begun in the Spirit,** are ye now made perfect by the flesh?

(Galatians 3:3)

The foolish deviates from the course.

Conclusion: Don't Blame God

King Ahab began in the Spirit, but he ended in the flesh. He changed lanes and things, of course, went south for him. His conscious was no longer righteous.

When things go south, we tend to blame God. However, when we litigate Ahab's situation by the scriptures, we find that God is not to be blamed; for He is never the problem. Being faithful, God dutifully released the grace needed for victory. And He also shared the blueprint recorded in heaven for that day. That included God's observation of Ahab's fall from grace. God observed the *upset* and commissioned the Prophet of God to share His findings with the king. God left out nothing that was profitable for Ahab. God shared: you will to go up, but you will also fall. You will turn from following Me and yield to a deceiving spirit. That spirit will cause Israel to be without a shepherd.

God released His grace to Ahab to empower him to stay the course. God knew that if Ahab were to *turn* to his flesh, his fall from grace would be fatal. This fatalness was primarily due to the fact that Ahab carried unforgiveness—a hatred that produces a root of bitterness. A turn would release all the corruption that he had sown to his flesh. But the choice was his.

King Ahab had embarked upon a breach-upon-breach course of action: He failed to *discern truth from falsehood*; instead he believed the lying spirits. He failed to *buy the field*; he did not receive the Word of the prophet with joy. He failed *to occupy* the Word that was sown in his heart; that Israel would be scattered. He failed to pray; he consistently confessed *doubt*. He failed to *dominate*; he bound the prophet of God. He failed to *watch*; he yielded to his emotions, saying, "I hate him." He *sowed to the flesh*; he disguised himself. Being weary, he failed to reap due season. He refused the contrary instruction and failed to fight back.

I Learned:

_____

_____

_____

_____

_____

_____

_____

_____

_____

_____

_____ .

These questions refer to the Conclusion in <u>this</u> workbook: **Conclusion: Don't Blame God.**

Read **'Conclusion: Don't Blame God'** in <u>this</u> workbook.

a.   Why did things 'go south' for King Ahab?

_____

_____

_____

b.   What did Ahab carry that led to his fall from grace?

_____

_____

_____

c.   List the Processes of Grace that Ahab failed to use to his advantage.

_____

_____

_____

_____

By faith …they shut the mouths of lions…

(Hebrews 11:33 NLT)

Give the right answer…answer discretely

Epilogue

Don't' Give the Wrong Answer

When my nephew was in elementary school, he began acting out. He had always been a good kid, but now he was in a new school and new environment. The school psychologist decided to test him, to see if he had any learning difficulties.

After administering the IQ test, the Dr. said, "I don't know what is wrong with him." He said, "I tested him and he scored in the high IQ range."

That evening I talked with my nephew and jokingly asked why he had scored so high on the intelligence test. His response echoes in my heart even today, after some 4o years later. He said, "I just could not put down the wrong answer."

It is only a test. When we are going through the tests and trials of life, our circumstances are not being tested, we are. We pass the test when we give the right answer. The enemy of our soul is searching to see if we will respond to the influence of grace or fail the test? In other words, will we fight back? After all, the Bible is an open book test.

The seven processes of grace will be met with answers affirming the Lordship of grace, or with answers in the negative, affirming the enemy of grace. The choice is ours.

I Learned:

Answers to Questions

For Cosmic Criminal: Chapters 1-6

Chapter 1: Grace vs. Perception
a. David offered Hanun unmerited kindness.
b. Hanun's case against grace was that he trusted his own perception.
c. When grace is disrupted it becomes a legal process that must be litigated by scripture.
d. A breach is created whenever we miss the mark.
e. The enemy says, in effect, it's their fault because they sinned and destroyed themselves.
f. 'King to king' business is God communicating with mature sons and daughters of the Kingdom of God.

Chapter 2: Grace vs. Unbelief
a. The man's case was that he <u>justified</u> his condition.
b. Unbelief is initially received when we believe something that God did not say.
c. Unbelief affects our conscience by putting us at odds with it.
d. The son decided to confront himself.
e. Factors that hinder the flow of grace are competing and contaminating influences of unbelief.

Chapter 3: Grace vs. Fear

a. Elijah's case against grace was that he felt threatened.
b. Jezebel was the wife of the wicked king of Israel. She had threatened to kill Elijah.

c. God redeemed Elijah by calling him by his name.

d. The angel called Gideon a mighty man of valor because Gideon responded to the influence of grace on his heart.

Chapter 4: Grace vs. Care

a. Martha's case against grace was that she had <u>legitimate care</u>.
b. Daniel's heart was not divided and that allowed him to remain faithful.

c. A 'flood attack' is one where cares, concerns, doubts, fears, and unbelief all beat vehemently upon our souls and minds.

d. Standing shows our position of power. It is important for us to 'stand' because it says that our hearts are established; that we are settled: not moved by evil tidings; just trusting God.

Chapter 5: Grace vs. Doubt

a. The author's case against grace was seeing the <u>difficulty of the task</u> at hand.

b. Some of the impacts of doubt on our minds are: asking questions, being hesitant, being undetermined, being slow to believe, horror, fear, dread, apprehension, suspicion; withholding confidence, distrust, withholding assent, wavering, and seeing the difficulty.

c. When we are bound by doubt, we are unable to partake of the deliverance that grace offers.

d. When doubt challenges areas where our abilities are untested, we tend to lean to our own understanding.

e. Doubt is resisted by faith.

Chapter 6: Grace vs. Pleasant Knowledge

a. Ammon's case against grace was that he had a <u>sense of entitlement</u>.

b. Tamar's 'way out' was for Ammon to, "…speak to the king; he will not withhold me from you."

c. Ammon refused Tamar's wisdom because his fleshly knowledge was more pleasant to him.

d. Pleasant knowledge is defined as anything that justifies the flesh, yet is contrary to your divine destiny.

Answers

For Cosmic Criminal: Chapter 7

Grace to Discern

a. Abraham first tapped into his spiritual inheritance by calling those things that be not as though they were. He called himself a father of multitudes while he was still childless.

b. Abraham accurately discerned the will of God when he said, "God will provide Himself a lamb for the burnt offering."

c. The heaven to earth agreement between God and Adam was when Adam realized that he did not see (*discern*) the creature that matched the name that he was discerning in his heart: Eve.

d. The 'calling and naming' component of grace refers to the guarding of our will.

e. Using his own fleshly wisdom, King Joash failed to discern the voice of the imposter from the voice of grace. That breach cost him the grace to consume the enemy.

f. The Lord said to the Israelites: "…if ye will not drive out the inhabitants of the land from before you; then it shall come to pass, that those which ye let remain of them shall be pricks in your eyes, and thorns in your sides,…"

Grace to Overcome

a. 'Buying and Selling' refers to buying the truth and not selling the truth.

b. Mary reasoned that if her spirit is rejoicing, she should rejoice as well; in as much as, a house divided cannot stand.

c. The wise virgins, following the influence of grace, bought extra oil. But the foolish did not.

d. The field is the ground where battles are fought; it consists of things that are contrary to us.

e. To buy the 'field' we must count it all joy. Joy buys the field, liberates it and gives us an immediate turnaround.

Grace to Occupy
a. Grace to Occupy focuses on the concept of occupying—where we (occupy) seize the Word that was sown in our hearts; *it is our reasonable service.*
b. The Rechabites obeyed and did according to all that Jonadab, their father, commanded them.
c. Hearers and doers act on the word, hearers only do not.
d. The man *neglected* to <u>keep</u> the Word that he had <u>heard</u> in his heart.
e. The man was negligence, which is a failure to perform the reasonable person standard.

Grace to Pray
a. Grace to Pray guards our faith. It focuses on *believing* we receive.
b. Doubt is the weapon the enemy uses against the grace to pray.
c. The fig tree tried to deceive Jesus using *doubt* (it made Him question his faith).
d. Jesus taught His disciples how to attack doubt by praying mountain moving prayers.
e. If we do not forgive others, God will not forgive us.
f. When we sin and miss the mark, <u>prayer</u> gives us all one more move.

Grace to Dominate

a. Grace to Dominate guards our minds. It focuses on our walk of <u>dominion</u>.

b. The woman was called "Loosed."

c. Without the kingdom of God, we all bow to the image of the fallen nature; this entity, known also as our <u>sin nature</u>, gives us a negative perception of life, ourselves, and of others.

d. Hebrews 12:14-15 says: "Follow peace with all men, and holiness…"

e. Binding and loosing involves binding the bad perception and loosing the good: *It fights against bitterness.*

Grace to Watch

a. Grace to Watch guards the heart. It focuses on being alert; *ready to fight back*!

b. The heroine of the movie fought back.

c. The man believed the old prophet and went <u>back</u> with him, disregarding God's commandment.

d. After his meal, he left and was slain by a lion. He lacked importunity in his watch.

Grace to Sow

a. David's men, being grieved, spoke of stoning <u>him</u>.

b. We will reap in 'due season' if we faint not.

c. Fainting will stop the harvest.

d. The last servant sowed to his flesh and could not reap the harvest that God had laid up for him from the foundation of the world.

Answers

For Cosmic Criminal: Chapter 8

Possessing Your Possessions

a. The Israelites' case against grace was that they were filled with dismay and fear.

b. After being accused by his brother, David had to show dominion over his own emotions.

c. The Israelites left God out of the equation.

d. The shout of a king is the shout of joy, triumph, and exultation.

Answers

For Cosmic Criminal Workbook- Conclusion

These answers refer to the Conclusion in <u>this</u> workbook: **Conclusion: Don't Blame God.**

a. Things went 'south' for Ahab because he began in the Spirit, but he ended in the flesh.

b. Ahab carried unforgiveness, a hatred that produces a root of bitterness.

c. He failed to *discern truth from falsehood*; instead he believed the lying spirits. He failed to *buy the field*; he did not receive the Word of the prophet with joy. He failed *to occupy* the Word that was sown in his heart; that Israel would be scattered. He failed to pray; he consistently confessed *doubt*. He failed to *dominate*; he bound the prophet of God. He failed to *watch*; he yielded to his emotions, saying, "I hate him." He *sowed to the flesh*; he disguised himself. Being weary, he failed to reap due season. He refused the contrary instruction and failed to fight back.

Thou therefore, my son, be strong in
the grace that is in Christ Jesus.

(2 Timothy 2:1)

Grace makes you strong

About the Authors

Carolyn Chambers is a licensed minister and a member of Faith Ministerial Alliance. She is a celebrated Christian author, and is best known for her groundbreaking work: *Discovering Your Anointing Numbers: Allow me to introduce you to Yourself.*

She and her husband, Keith, have also developed Anointing Profiles that yield personalized commentaries based on birth demographics.

Carolyn holds a Bachelor's degree from the University of Wisconsin and a Master's degree from the University of Arizona.

Keith holds a Bachelor's degree from Loyola University of Chicago. They live in Phoenix, Arizona, with their two sons: Nehemiah and Zacharias. They are members of Pilgrim Rest Baptist Church.

Other Books by Carolyn Chambers

DISCOVERING YOUR ANOINTING NUMBERS

Carolyn Chambers

In her life-changing new book, Carolyn Chambers helps readers discover their anointing numbers and empower them to fight life's great battle-themselves. Simply put—everyone is at war with *self*. But walking anointed is something everyone can achieve.

In, "Discovering Your Anointing Numbers: Allow me to introduce you to Yourself," Carolyn Chambers examines the influence that birth demographics have on human behavior. This is a compelling read for all.

THE ANOINTED LIFE-

Crucifying the Flesh

Carolyn Chambers

The Anointed Life: **Powerful New Book by Celebrated Christian Author Proves Flesh is the True "Enemy of the Soul"**

Everyone faces adversity and tests in life but some pass where others fail. While faith and the word of God explain why these patterns exist, millions still search for answers. In her compelling new book, the author exposes the true enemy of the soul – the flesh. "Simply put," she says, "everybody is at war with themselves."

THE LORD'S PRAYER --REVISITED

7 WAYS TO DELIVERENCE

Carolyn Chambers

Praying the Lord's Prayer is the Answer

Understanding The Lord's Prayer is the Solution!

Understanding is the key to whether we have solutions in life or just answers. The Lord's Prayer – Revisited gives us the understanding we need to examine the enemy's front line of offense: self—and its undercover role in the attacks against our lives. The Lord's Prayer disrupts the plans of the wicked and scatters the enemy of our soul **seven** *ways*.

THE COSMIC CRIMINAL

THE CASE AGAINST GRACE

Carolyn Chambers

We have heard of an eye for an eye, and a tooth for a tooth, but God offers us grace for grace. Grace empowers us to possess our possessions. There are no losers. However, the kingdom does operate by laws. As law-abiding citizens, we prosper until we breach the process of grace and become: Cosmic Criminals.

www.ingramcontent.com/pod-product-compliance
Lightning Source LLC
Chambersburg PA
CBHW050445010526
44118CB00013B/1691